D1037033

The

Magic

begins with

50
Walt Disney
Parks & Resorts

ME

Class of 1955–2005

A Happiest Celebration On Earth Keepsake

The following are some of the trademarks of Disney Enterprises, Inc.: Adventureland, Audio-Animatronics®, Big Thunder Mountain Railroad, Critter Country, Disney, Disney Cruise Line Services, Disneyland Resort, Disneyland Resort Paris, Disney's Animal Kingdom Theme Park, Disney's Blizzard Beach Water Park, Disney's California Adventure Park, Disney's Grand Californian Hotel, Disney's Typhoon Lagoon Water Park, Epcot®, ESPN, Fantasyland, FASTPASS, Fort Wilderness, Frontierland, Hong Kong Disneyland Park, Imagineering, Imagineers, It's A Small World, Main Street, U.S.A., Mickey's Toontown, Monorail, New Orleans Square, Space Mountain, Splash Mountain, Tokyo Disney Resort, Tokyo DisneySea, Tomorrowland, Walt Disney World Resort.

Captain EO © Disney/Lucasfilm, Ltd.
Indiana Jones™ Adventure and Star Tours © Disney/Lucasfilm, Ltd.
Star Wars © Lucasfilm, Ltd
Roger Rabbit characters © Walt Disney Pictures/Amblin Entertainment
TARZAN'S TREEHOUSE®
TARZAN™ owned by Edgar Rice Burroughs, Inc. and used by permission.
Winnie the Pooh characters based on the "Winnie the Pooh" works by A.A. Milne and E.H. Shepard.
Toy Story characters © Disney Enterprises, Inc./Pixar Animation Studios

Sponsors depicted are not necessarily representative of current Disneyland sponsors.

Project Manager: Roxanne Robert

Disney Editions
Wendy Lefkon, Editorial Director
Jody Revenson, Editor

A Camphor Tree Book
Bruce Gordon, Designer

Project Consultant: Jeff Kurtti

First Edition, 2005

ISBN 0-7868-3906-6

The following abbreviations are used throughout the book:

DLR	Disneyland Resort	DCL	Disney Cruise Line
WDW	Walt Disney World Resort	HKDL	Hong Kong Disneyland Resort
TDR	Tokyo Disney Resort	WDTC	Walt Disney Travel Co., Inc.
DLRP	Disneyland Resort Paris	WDI	Walt Disney Imagineering

TABLE OF CONTENTS

Walt Disney Parks and Resorts

James A. Rasulo
President

July 17, 2005

Dear Fellow Cast Members,

It is with enormous pride and thanks that I write to you on the occasion of the 50th anniversary of the opening of Disneyland. *Pride* that with your help, we have been able to uphold the ideals of our founder, Walt Disney, for 50 years; and *thanks* because through your efforts and dedication, we have been able to grow Walt's "idea" into a business that is today the leading family entertainment destination on three continents.

No one knows better than I how difficult a job this has been, and what an important role our Cast Members, across the decades and now the world, have played in our success. In creating the magic for our Guests every day, there are few "starring roles." But as a nearly 20-year Cast Member myself, I know, as all of you do, that being a Disney Cast Member is one of the most satisfying jobs there is.

Being a representative of the greatest and most beloved cultural entity of the past century —whether in a front line or a backstage role—is both a great responsibility and an enormous joy. We know that what we do impacts people in a truly tangible and authentic way.

At Disney we create an encompassing sense of occasion—so much so that for our Guests, their Disney experience becomes part of their personal culture, the collective memory of their family and friends. It is something they treasure, praise, celebrate, and pass on to others.

But perhaps the most important reason for our success is the ability to involve our Guests in a story—one in which they participate.

This book is my gift to you, in commemoration of the Happiest Celebration On Earth, and in recognition and appreciation of the unique contribution that you make to Disney. We would not be here except for you. You are the reason our Guests love us. Within these pages we have assembled a tribute to **you**, and to your forerunners, and a testimonial to an unparalleled half-century of excellence, as well as to the remarkable future that waits for us at Walt Disney Parks and Resorts.

Disney magic is reality for millions of people around the world and for generations to come because of **you**, your belief in our purpose, and your pride in what you do.

Jay

500 South Buena Vista Street / Burbank, California 91521-1050 / 818-560-4200 / Fax 818-845-2693

Part of the Magic of The Walt Disney Company   © Disney

Walt Disney Imagineering
1401 Flower St
Glendale, CA 91221

Our half-century tradition of sharing smiles lives on in you.

"You can dream, create, design, and build the most wonderful place in the world, but it takes people to make the dream a reality."
—Walt Disney

The role of "Cast Member" in the Disney show began with Walt Disney himself, even before Disneyland Park opened a half century ago. People often commented on "The Disney Touch," a certain quality that seemed inherent in all of Disney's work, from films to comic books to music. "The secret is teamwork," Walt said plainly. And from that plain-spoken ideal, a half-century tradition of excellence began.

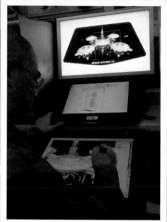

A Special Place Needs Special People

In the making of his films and television programs, Walt Disney was an exceptional storyteller, a great innovator, and a visionary. One of his greatest but most-overlooked skills was team building: knowing how to assemble the right coalition of talents and personalities to achieve a particular goal. Disneyland continued and evolved his team-building ideas.

Initially, Walt trusted others to cast the roles in the Disneyland show. "The first year I leased out the parking concession," he recalled, "brought in the usual security guards—things like that—but I soon realized my mistake. I couldn't have outside help and still put over my idea of hospitality. So now we recruit and train every one of our employees."

Walt knew that Disneyland was a unique enterprise. The people who lived and worked there every day would have to be a cohesive team of unique people.

December 6, 2004

Dear Disney Cast Members:

We recently visited the Mouse's house (Disneyland and California Adventure) and I must let you all know the stupendous job you all do, and just how much you are appreciated.

I know that many of you are there because this is your job. You are working because your tuition is due, the mortgage is high, you're working to care for your family, this is what you get up and do every day, but to this Mom, you are all kind, wonderful and magical people, and a gift to my son.

My son, William, is a special needs child; this basically means he processes the world differently than other 'normal' children. Change can sometimes be difficult for William, and he has to warm up to new concepts. He has difficulty talking, and mostly communicates through sign language or a picture exchange communications system (P.E.C.S).

For us to visit Disneyland was a great undertaking to say the least. We spend every dime we have on our son's medical needs, so there is not a lot left over. It took us a year to fill up the change jar, and we sold anything we could to make this trip happen.

We had to stay for several days so William could take in the parks a little at a time so he would never get over stimulated and bring on a seizure. We needed a room to overlook the park so he could see where he was going, so he would not be frightened. The room needed to be close to the park so we could take our son back to the room regularly for breaks so he would not be overstressed. The staff at the Paradise Pier bent over backwards to accommodate our needs. The concierge staff, Christina and Donny, were wonderful, and so very kind. I am not used to feeling special but I really appreciated it.

My son was having such a great time at the park, and he was learning! William started to TALK. He verbalized constantly, something he had not been doing. He was doing well with the crowds, and not showing any signs of fear. We bit the bullet and extended our stay by a day. I was afraid we would have to move rooms, which would upset our son, but the front desk staff, Christina, and the manager, did a lot of juggling to allow us to stay in our room, which meant so much to us, and made our lives so much easier.

From the time we made our reservations to our departure, everything was perfect. I was so overwhelmed that my son was happy due to the Cast Members going the extra step. The staff made my life easier, where I was actually relaxed, and I had forgotten what that had felt like.

The Disney park staff was amazing!! I know to them this was just another day on the job, but they touched the life of a beautiful four year old boy, who hugged Goofy! Days earlier he would not have done this. Goofy went out of his way, being so gentle with my son…he was a friend to a little boy who had no friends. Goofy is now his best friend, and he tells everyone how Goofy hugged him.

Again the Cast Members did not know the huge accomplishment my son had made on that day, but my husband and I had tears in our eyes. The time you take to recognize a child and single

DONNY MARROCHE,
DISNEY'S PARADISE PIER HOTEL FRONT DESK (DLR)
"I try to make every Guest interaction magical and I follow the golden rule… never forget a Guest's name."

CHRISTINE DURALDE,
DISNEY'S PARADISE PIER HOTEL GUEST SERVICES (DLR)
"I strive to create magical memories for our Guests by exceeding their expectations and creating a friendly atmosphere."

him out may be the highlight of his young life. My son gained so much from his Disneyland experience; he learned more in a few days we were there than the months he has had of physical, occupational, and speech therapy.

William was a lonely child who did not have any friends, but now he has so many new friends, such as Mickey, Goofy, the Pooh gang, Bear in the Big Blue House, Stanley, Roly Poly Olie, Flick and Atta, they are all real!

The magic of Disney was evident on our visit, it truly is the happiest place on earth, because William laughed, giggled, talked, and made friends, and most importantly he did not want to go to the safety of home. William ventured out, and wanted to stay at the 'Mouse's House.' William actually cried when we left Disneyland, normally he would have wanted to go home…the magic of Disney.

My son uses sign language and every morning since we returned home, as he awakes holding his Goofy, he signs to me 'go to the Mouse's house,' I smile and say yes we will go back to the mouse's house soon. I will do whatever it takes to get my son back to the happiest place on Earth, next year. I am already adding to the coin jar!! Thank you, and know that you all are loved, and in my prayers, and that you all do make a difference in people's lives. We will see you all next year, just look for the proud mom and dad with their beautiful little boy.

Thank you!

Dorothy, Bill, and William Sullivan

August 8, 2002

Mr. Michael Eisner, CEO
Walt Disney Company
500 South Buena Vista St.
Burbank, CA 91521

Dear Mr. Eisner,

I'm sure it comes as no surprise to you, that not all of God's Angels' are in Heaven. In fact some of them are actually located in Disneyland.

My 4 1/2-year-old granddaughter, Natalie, was the recipient of a "wish" from the Make A Wish Foundation. On the day of our arrival, your cast member Suzanne Mukogawa befriended me. She immediately took on the role of one of Disneyland's Angels. During our conversation, she was made aware of Natalie's condition and prognosis.

It is nearly miraculous what transpired over the next three days in the way of a support network that Suzanne put together. The outpouring of love and concern from so many members of the Disney Family was extremely thoughtful and caring. Natalie received a number of souvenir gifts and get-well greetings. Your artist, Tom Kelly, personally offered a complimentary caricature and presented a gift for Natalie that was specially selected for her.

I will never forget a crowning moment, just as we were leaving. As fate would have it, Goofy was coming through the lobby at the same time and spent a few very precious moments with our little Granddaughter.

The extra time, energy, and concern shown by Suzanne, Tom, Arwen and Disneyland's other Angels made Natalie's stay so much more enjoyable and meaningful.

I wish I had a completely happy ending, but our dearest Natalie passed away on June 27th and joined the other Angels.

I have always believed in the magic of Disneyland and the wonderful spell that Disneyland can cast. As a result of the love and caring your Cast Members show, I also believe in *Disneyland's* Angels. Please pass along my special love and eternal thanks to Suzanne, Tom, Arwen and all of your wonderful staff.

With all my sincerest appreciation,

Betty Wyant

Betty L. Wyant

"After having been through Disneyland, I am certain that when Mr. Walt Disney met Saint Peter, he was told, 'Just the man I've been waiting for. We need someone up here to set up a "Heaven" for children!'"
—Disneyland Guest
July 1, 1969

SUZANNE MUKOGAWA, CULINARY HOSTESS (DLR)
"What Walt created is a phenomenal thing and I am proud to be a part of it. It is all about the children, that is what we are here for."

We recently returned from our third Disney cruise — we first sailed on the Magic in October 2002, then on the Wonder in November, 2003, and then again on the Magic when we left Port Canaveral on October 9. This last week-long cruise was one of the absolute best vacations we've ever had! The Magic is incredible and the crew is just plain awesome!

Our cabin steward, Nilo, was extremely efficient—his special touches and extraordinary efforts ensured that our cabin was absolutely perfect and we were most comfortable. On our first day, we asked for a bucket of ice and each day after that—morning and evening—we had ice. When we came back on board after getting caught in rain at Castaway Cay, Nilo had two huge fresh towels folded and waiting for us. If he saw us coming down the hallway, he opened our stateroom door for us. He was never intrusive, but always available, taking very good care of our room.

Our dinner servers, Uri and Ana, were great! They took great effort to make sure the menus were explained and our dinners were served promptly. (And, the food was delicious!) They remembered our favorites and quickly and sweetly took care of every need.

Our week was also highlighted by the outstanding, friendly, and accommodating services of Sandra and Benita (in Preludes and also on desk during the sail-away party). They were very friendly, conversational, interesting, and efficient. These Crew Members are truly assets to the Disney Cruise Line and we only wish that we could sail again tomorrow with the same excellent folks who became our 'friends' by the end of the week.

Quite frankly, there aren't enough words to express our utmost satisfaction and gratitude for a week that was truly 'magical.' Thanks to all! Hopefully, we sail again soon!

from Cathy & Ralph Tack

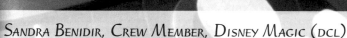

SANDRA BENIDIR, CREW MEMBER, DISNEY MAGIC (DCL)
"I really love talking with the Guests onboard. I help them relax and enjoy their time with us. I am proud of the job we do—making people happy all day—that is what we do. I love our Guests!"

BENITA CULZAC
CREW MEMBER, DISNEY MAGIC (DCL)
"I love everything about my job. The best part of my role is when I make a drink for a Guest and they keep coming back to me for another perfect drink."

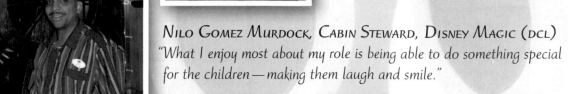

NILO GOMEZ MURDOCK, CABIN STEWARD, DISNEY MAGIC (DCL)
"What I enjoy most about my role is being able to do something special for the children—making them laugh and smile."

Dear Mr. Disney:

What prompted me to write to you is to compliment you on the outstanding personnel which you have assembled to operate this tremendous project. Each person enacted their part—not only to make us feel welcome, but to set the stage so we were oriented into the overall fantasy of Disneyland. Everywhere we were greeted with smiling courtesy and were made to feel that everything was done for our individual pleasure. Such loyalty to you and to the spirit of Disneyland is rarely found in employees these days. It is a tremendous tribute to you, for these fine people really make Disneyland a living thing instead of merely an unusual amusement park.

R. Baggott, December 23, 1955

ORLANDO SANTOS, STATEROOM HOST, DISNEY MAGIC (DCL)

"In 1972 my family drove here from Chicago for our vacation and we camped at Fort Wilderness. The incredible Guest service we received is what inspired me to choose a career with the Walt Disney Company, 'The Happiest Place on Earth to work!' After 15 years of employment, the pixie dust has not gone away. At the end of each day if I have made a difference in someone's life by creating a magical memory, I know that my life and what I do has true purpose."

"My wife and I have never been on a cruise before (despite our 50 years of age), and actually were not enthusiastic about it at all. How wrong we were! We have never been on a more relaxing vacation! The process to board and de-board, the crew and staff, and the experience we had were OUTSTANDING! I have never felt so special in my life. I have never been looked after in such a caring manner before. I have never met so many people who work with the public everyday that showed such enthusiasm and flexibility to meet the guests' needs. So much so, that when it came to leave the ship after 7 days, I actually felt like crying. I didn't want to leave these people who I now considered my friends! **Orlando** kept our stateroom spotless and always in perfect condition. His creative creations with bath towels made coming back to the room a wondrous experience all on its own! Although he never spoke very long to us in any one conversation, his attention to the smallest details in our room reflected his commitment to us, his guests.

"Thank you, Disney Cruise Line, in providing a wonderful experience! I watched in awe of so many focused individuals doing their best to ensure a pleasant and safe environment for my family and I to enjoy ourselves. I have spoken very highly of your efforts to everyone at work, church, and in my many social contacts—if you are going on a cruise, go Disney! My wife and I hope to go on another Disney Cruise in the near future, thanks to the staff and crew of the Disney Magic!"

—Barry L. Spink

MARIANNE HUNNEL, FOOD AND BEVERAGE EDUCATIONAL CONSULTANT (WDW)

DAVID WASSERMAN

To whom it may concern,

I wanted to give my sincere thanks to one of your exemplary employees, named Dorothy Heck, from the Chicago ESPN Zone.

After an exhausting flight across country, I wanted to relax and watch football with a group of customers. There was a big wait and I became frustrated. Dorothy proceeded to come out, greet us and get us seated in a timely fashion.

She was cordial and efficient. I wish I could find an employee like her to work at *my* place of business. She turned a potentially frustrating situation into an extremely enjoyable experience. I travel on business a great deal and it is rare to find such great service.

Thank you, Dorothy, for a great day.

DW

DOROTHY HECK,
ESPN ZONE (CHICAGO)
"Mr. Wasserman and his group were so enthusiastic about visiting ESPN Zone, I could not help but try to find a way to make their day special. They were so happy and appreciative; they even invited me to visit them in Florida as we shared stories about my favorite team—the Miami Dolphins!"

"A wonderful thing just happened. I brought my sister to Tokyo Disneyland so that she could have a good time. We wanted to buy some cookies but entered the wrong store. A young man in a security uniform kindly told us where we needed to go. When I used sign language to tell my sister what he said, he started signing to her too! She soon became happy—happier in fact, than I've seen her in the last two years. I never even thought that someone who works at Disneyland might know sign language. Disneyland, you never disappoint us! For me, as well as my sister, today has been a terrific day. Thanks very much to that young man and to everyone at Disneyland!"

東京ディズニーリゾートゲスト

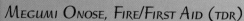

RIE FUKUI, CAST DEVELOPMENT (TDR)
"When working in the Cast Activities Center, I strive to support the Cast so they will enjoy their jobs and share their enthusiasm and happiness with our Guests."

MEGUMI ONOSE, FIRE/FIRST AID (TDR)
"I provide magic for our Guests by ensuring that they have a safe and happy visit to our Resort without ever realizing our presence."

KELLY BEAGAN, DOORMAN, DISNEY'S HOTEL NEW YORK (DLRP)
"I always keep in mind that I am the first and last image a Guest will have of their stay. Every little detail counts."

PAULO MACHADO, BELLMAN
DISNEY'S HOTEL NEW YORK
(DLRP)
"Relax and enjoy...let me carry the load!"

FRANCK CHAFFARDON,
CONCIERGE, DISNEY'S HOTEL NEW YORK (DLRP)
"I believe in assisting and informing our Guests beyond their expectations — from a simple smile to the organization of a complete stay, nothing is too much."

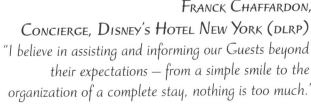

21-1-02

Dear Disneyland Paris:

I am writing to you as a result of a recent transaction with your company. As a management consultant and people skills specialist I tend to automatically assess any business or service of which I am a consumer. I have yet to find a business that could surprise me; however, my experience with your company was a massive shock.

I was wanting to book a visit to Disney at very short notice and being a businessman tend to be in a hurry and do not look forward to dealing with the usual (my preconceived ideas) automated telephone queuing system and poorly trained sales persons, who are usually very unhelpful and disinterested.

The employees who assisted me were very bright and pleasant and extremely efficient. I remember thinking 'God' what is happening; people are actually paying attention here. I have yet to receive such friendly, efficient service ever before in my life, I am still shell-shocked.

In my work I see lots of businesses not getting it right, so it was a real unexpected pleasure to find people paying attention in the way your staff did. I have also seen the Disney customer care (training) videos and know that Disney are world-leaders in customer service and maintain very high standards.

I felt as if I really mattered and my business with your company was valued. My inquiry was quite a complicated one and your staff answered all of my questions efficiently and accurately, and went out of their way to satisfy my needs.

Yours sincerely,

D. Elliott

"You have created something very special, every single Disney person we met lived the magic, we have never experienced such a willingness to meet and exceed our every need. I own a service business myself and it is therefore incredible to me that a business your size can achieve the passion and dedication of each and everyone on your staff.

"Please, please, please pass on our heartfelt thanks to your whole team, but in particular your team at the Disney Hotel Castle Club. Our children had a wonderful time and your experience will live in their childhood dreams forever!"

David, Sarah, Elliott, and Emilia Beattie
Disneyland Paris Guests
October, 2002

July 2, 2004

To Pop Century Front Desk Manager:

I just wanted to drop you a note and tell you what a fantastic experience our family had at your newest Disney World Resort during our stay beginning on June 24th. Not only were the grounds and facilities immaculate as always, but once again your "Cast Members" were warm, friendly and as always extremely happy and courteous.

It all began with the enthusiastic reception we received when we checked in at the front desk. Cast Member Michael Manzella greeted us so warmly and couldn't have been more knowledgeable and gracious in explaining all the various nuances of the resort. He helped us plan out our day, explained all the tickets to us, and when we mentioned going to eat somewhere, immediately started explaining different restaurants we could go to all over the property and offered to make us Priority Seating. It might have had to do with the fact that we come from the same city that he does, which he commented on several times during hour conversation.

The next day, we went to the parks and had an amazing time, and when we went to our room thinking the fun was over, we realized that it had just begun! When we walked into our room, what a wonderful surprise we received, a basket full of goodies proclaiming us "Family of the Day." This was great for the kids who got to keep that Disney "adrenaline rush" going even after we got back from a great and exhausting day. I think this truly made our short, but sweet trip, very special.

The next day as I walked through the lobby, I saw Michael once again and told him I had a great time and thanked him. He not only remembered me by name, but asked how Nicky and Anthony enjoyed the park and toys from the basket. Naturally I said they loved them (who wouldn't?) and I had to run because everyone was in the car ready to go. As I was leaving, he shook my hand and said "Don't forget to say Hello to Hollywood for me."

It was really special for us to have someone take out the extra time in their day to make sure everything was settled and enjoyable for us. Michael by far did this, and exceeded our greatest expectations. He should be commended for his great guest service.

Once again, our Disney experience was awesome. On behalf of my entire family, Nicky, Anthony and Cristina, we thank you all.

Sincerely,

John S. Anfuso
Hollywood, FL 33021

MICHAEL MANZELLA, FRONT DESK,
DISNEY'S POP CENTURY RESORT (WDW)
*"My philosophy is something
Rudy Giuliani said,
'Over-deliver in your service!'"*

HOLLY LONG, SALES HOSTESS, DISNEY'S YACHT CLUB RESORT (WDW)

"I want every Guest, especially the children, to be overcome by a sense of 'specialness'—as if they are the only Guests."

Guest.mail@wdw.disneyonline.com

Dear Madam/Sir,

We want to thank all of the Cast Members at WDW for another incredible experience. Our recent trip makes trip number 5 to WDW since 1994 for our family.

We stayed at the Yacht Club and on our final night, our youngest son, Alex, age 8, was in tears upon our return from Magic Kingdom to the hotel – he was so sad to be leaving. We had to pick up a delivery in the gift shop. While there, Holly asked Alex if he was okay. I told her that he was sad to be leaving. Holly visited with us and tried to make Alex feel better. We went to our room only to receive a phone call. The caller said that Mickey Mouse heard there was a sad, little boy in our room and asked if it would be okay if Mickey had a friend deliver a special package to him. Moments later, Holly appeared at our door with a care package complete with a little Mickey, toys and candy. Since Alex was in the shower when Holly arrived, he is convinced that Mickey must have actually come to our room. These gifts remain in prominent places in Alex's room at home.

Thank you WDW for keeping the magic and for not changing the fairy tale adventures. How refreshing to be able to use one's imagination and not a computer joy stick! Again – thanks to Holly, the Yacht Club and WDW!

Julie Karavas
Lincoln, NE

The Simple Things

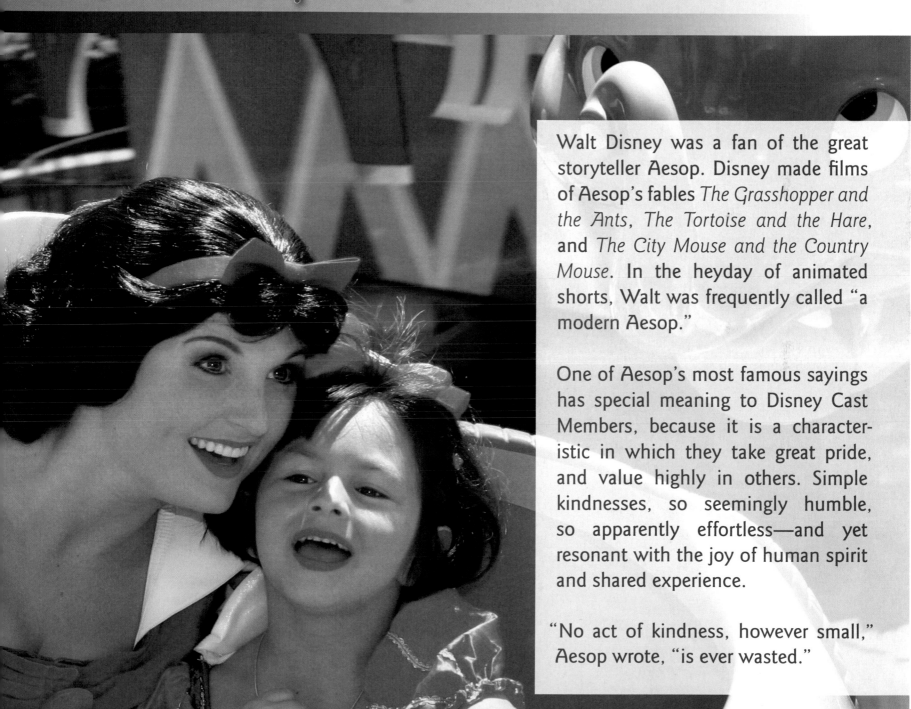

Walt Disney was a fan of the great storyteller Aesop. Disney made films of Aesop's fables *The Grasshopper and the Ants*, *The Tortoise and the Hare*, and *The City Mouse and the Country Mouse*. In the heyday of animated shorts, Walt was frequently called "a modern Aesop."

One of Aesop's most famous sayings has special meaning to Disney Cast Members, because it is a characteristic in which they take great pride, and value highly in others. Simple kindnesses, so seemingly humble, so apparently effortless—and yet resonant with the joy of human spirit and shared experience.

"No act of kindness, however small," Aesop wrote, "is ever wasted."

Disneyland Paris
Boite postale 110
F-77777 Marne-la-Vallee, Cedex 4
France
ATTN: Mr. Thion

Dear Mr. Thion:

We feel we must write to you to praise Castle Club Manageress Chantale Leroux regarding how extremely helpful she was to our daughter Holly.

We arranged for our daughter to have a very special 18th birthday at Disney with her close friends and to stay in Castle Club. Chantale went out of her way to make Holly's birthday extra special, even arranging a birthday surprise for her in the Lounge. She did so much for us and nothing was too much trouble and consequentially, my daughter was given a birthday she will remember all her life.

We have visited Disney since the park opened and stayed in Castle Club (we did meet you briefly before our departure in December last year) and can only praise Chantale for her helpfulness. She makes sure our needs are always met as we 'drive her mad' before we arrive. We joke with her about this and she always makes sure our stay is wonderful – it's always a pleasure to return to Disney.

Yours Sincerely,

Lester and Linda Tilbury

Lester & Linda Tilbury
Essex, England

CHANTALE LEROUX, CASTLE CLUB (DLRP)
"I always strive for perfection and Guest satisfaction. The sky is the limit to please our Guests and make the Disney magic happen."

Susan Paige, Sales Service Specialist (WDTC)
"Simply stated, my philosophy is to treat the Guests like family members."

We recently returned from a wonderful week at Disneyland. I wanted to let you know how nice it was to work with the Walt Disney Travel Company. Three days before our departure date, my father passed away.

My family encouraged us to try and keep our vacation on track, so I called Disney Travel to see if I could get some flights changed and change a few other items. The staff was so wonderful, they helped find a different flight, cancelled what needed to be, and expressed deep regret for our loss. **Susan** really helped out, even though it was at the last minute.

Everyone I have had contact with has been so great. Our trip was great, and a very nice change after all our sorrow. I just had to write and thank you for your wonderful staff, and all the nice things they did for my family.

Thank you,
Teresa, Anthony, Daniel, and Benjamin Winter
Via e-mail

Silvia Dias, Hotel Santa Fe (DLRP)

"It was probably just a typical scene, but I was simply touched by the Cast Member's warm smile, quick action, and above all, the act of interacting with the child by kneeling down at eye level of the child. Thank you very much."
—*Tokyo Disneyland Guest,*
After witnessing a Cast Member assist
a small child who had fallen

Dear Santa Fe Hotel:

As someone who has worked in the hotel industry for the last thirteen years, I know that the quality and strengths of the hotel operation tend to shine through in times of crisis—in which case you clearly have a very strong and high quality hotel property of which you should be truly proud.

—*Vicki Thomas, UK*

Paul Schrecongost

Walt Disney World Guest Communications
P.O. Box 10,400
Lake Buena Vista, FL 32830

To Whom It May Concern:

Overall, my stay at *Disney's Port Orleans* Resort was terrific; but one incident demands special attention. My family and I boarded a bus bound for *Epcot*. As the bus traveled down the road, my little girls realized they had forgotten their kid's activity passport for the different countries in *Epcot*. Since this was our last day in *Epcot*, they needed them desperately.

I walked up to the driver, explained my problem, and asked him if he was returning to Port Orleans after dropping off at the park. The driver, **Gabriel Pritz**, said he wasn't sure; but he would check into it and let me know. No sooner than I returned to my seat, **Gabriel** made an announcement: "If you folks don't mind and if nobody has to be some place at a certain time, would you mind if we swing back around to French Quarter to drop off a passenger." Nobody objected, except me. I bolted to the front and told **Gabriel** he didn't have to do that. I would simply wait for the next bus at *Epcot* to return me to Port Orleans. He said, "Nonsense, I had to swing by that way anyway."

The point of this long-winded dissertation is this:
your employees are amazing, and they are the primary reason we keep returning and will continue to return to Disney World year after year.
Also, please forward this to the proper channels to give special kudos to **Gabriel**; he didn't have to do what he did. And that's something my family will always remember. It's employees like **Gabriel** that make your "magic" happen.

Sincerely,

Paul

Paul Schrecongost
Pittsburgh, Pennsylvania

GABRIEL PRITZ, BUS DRIVER (WDW)
"I love to have fun with the Guests and I have a blast interacting with them. In my experience, when I can make the bus ride feel like anything other than just riding a bus, I have succeeded!"

"We want you to know how pleased we were with everything. Disneyland itself is wonderful. But we were particularly impressed by the little things."

—Mrs. Vern Birney
July 30, 1963

"Your employees, whether taken singly or all together, are extremely courteous indeed. They observe all the niceties. They, in addition to being efficient, very often take the time to pleasantly banter with, or simply smile at, the children. With very good wishes for continued success."

—W. Ryan, August 14, 1967

CHARLES FRANCISCO (FARLEY THE FIDDLER) (DLR)
"I create Disney magic with my fiddle and my feet!"

"We want you to know how much we enjoyed **Farley**, the fiddle-player entertaining the people waiting in line for Splash Mountain. We had a wonderful time listening to his music and his jokes. He was so personable and really seemed to go out of his way to make the people in the surrounding area feel welcome. It was fun to watch him interact with the crowd, and to share his enthusiasm and sense of humor."

—Rayna Litzenberger
Disneyland Guest, January 27, 2003

LINDA TOMA-OKAMOTO, FRONT DESK,
DISNEY'S GRAND CALIFORNIAN HOTEL (DLR)
"I truly believe that the 'magic' of Disney begins with every Cast Member and we have the unique ability to create memories for our Guests that will last a lifetime."

JEFF JAQUEZ, GOLDEN VINE WINERY (DLR)

TERI ROSS, GOLDEN VINE WINERY (DLR)

Debbie Newmeyer

Disneyland Resort
Guest Relations
P.O. Box 3232
Anaheim, CA 92803-3232

October 23, 2004

Dear Sirs:

"It was that most fun we've ever had at Disneyland!" "It was the best Birthday Party ever!" These were some of the comments I received after my girlfriends attended a 50th Birthday Party (10/8/04) for one of our dearest friends. Our theme was a princess party, and we choose Snow White. Granted our princess was 50, but she looked every bit the part in her red headband and Snow White cape!

I just had to write to tell you that this party could have never happened if it wasn't for your fantastic crew over at California Adventure/Golden Vine Winery. I was working with Xavier Plascencia, and he did an exceptional job for us! From the start he was professional and handled everything we asked for. We started our day at 12:30 with a wine and cheese reception. Everything was presented beautifully, and all the girls (16 of us!) were very impressed. Then off we went on a scavenger hunt through the two parks (I'm afraid they may still be telling stories about our group!).

Four hours later, completely exhausted, we returned to the Golden Vine for dinner at 6:30 pm., where we were all treated as princesses by your staff. I want to commend Jeff Jaquez, Javier Tovar, and Teri Ross. They waited on us hand and foot, literally, as they found band-aids for the blisters that we had gotten running through the two parks all day! I believe it was Javier Tovar that presented Deb (our birthday Snow White) with a special "poison apple" drink, which started the evening and made her feel so special.

Believe me; I know it's not easy to take care of 16, loud excited and exhausted women! Your staff should receive extra kudos for all their help, patience and great attitudes!

Thanks again to everyone that helps make your two resorts, the happiest place on earth!

Sincerely,

Debbie Newmeyer

Debbie Newmeyer
(The Evil Queen)
Newport Beach, CA

JAVIER TOVAR, GOLDEN VINE WINERY (DLR)

Xavier Plascencia
Golden Vine Winery (DLR)

*"Due to a series of tragic events in the life of
the 'birthday girl,' we worked together as a
team to make this a very special celebration
that would lift her spirits and leave her with
magical memories. The group was fun to
work with and we all felt good about creating
happiness — which is the most rewarding part
of our roles."*

"My sister had heard rumors about the special treatment birthday people received while at the park and without hesitation she told Linda at the front desk that it was our dad's, my daughter's, and my birthday that week.

"We caught an 8:00 p.m. dinner at the Storytellers Cafe. Our waiter, **Errol**, immediately noticed our birthday badges and insisted we have the mousse, and before dinner! I was tickled that my daughter was getting this special treatment and to my surprise he brought three plates for each of us birthday guests along with an entourage to sing 'Happy Birthday' to all of us. That was so sweet, and so unexpected. It topped the evening and is a memory I'll cherish and share with everyone I know."

Lara Martin
Disney's Grand Californian Hotel Guest, December 2004

Errol Vander Heyde, Culinary Server (DLR)
"I treat my Guests as I would like to be treated."

2004/05/12

Dear Tokyo Disneyland,

We were taking a picture of a hidden Mickey we found on the ground outside of the Lost River Outfitters when a female cast member said, "There's another hidden Mickey here." She did not reveal the exact location, but simply said, "It's in the direction I am facing now," like a game so that when we found it we would feel a sense of accomplishment. This actually seemed to be a difficult Mickey to find and even people who know about many hidden Mickeys did not know about this one. I have been to the park many times but I have not felt this happy in a long while, and I am impressed with the great cast members.

As we were taking a picture of this hidden Mickey, a custodial cast member noticed us and complimented us for finding it and took our picture with the hidden Mickey. We were only expecting to get a picture of the hidden Mickey, but we got a wonderful picture thanks to this cast member. We were especially grateful because he told us of yet another hidden Mickey as well. I hope next time we can be the ones to show others where the hidden Mickeys are. Thank you for a wonderful memory!

Y.H. – 東京

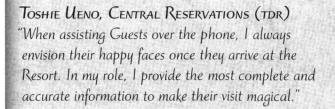

TOSHIE UENO, CENTRAL RESERVATIONS (TDR)
"When assisting Guests over the phone, I always envision their happy faces once they arrive at the Resort. In my role, I provide the most complete and accurate information to make their visit magical."

Dear Minnie:

The moment you saw us you came rushing over to shake our hands and even rubbing your cheek against my father's not-so-pretty face. I thanked you over and over again, but you stayed with us all the way to the exit. My father and I were very moved. Disneyland takes good care of its Guests. It was truly a memorable day.

—Tokyo Disneyland Guest

GARY LANDRUM, SHOW AWARENESS (WDI)

"Walt Disney Imagineering consists of writers, artists, programmers, librarians, and many other disciplines—yet, we're all storytellers. In fact, storytelling is the one role that all Disney Cast Members share. Disney Legend John Hench once said, 'The essence of good storytelling is to evoke emotion in the audience.' As a little boy growing up in Los Angeles, I remember the emotional thrill of visiting Disneyland—my sisters, brother, and I never wanted to go home!

"It also felt like a fantasy when we moved to Florida in the 1970s and I joined the Walt Disney World Cast. As a 16-year-old attractions host, I helped make the magic for Guests and really enjoyed doing it.

"Today, I lead the WDI-FL Show Awareness program, researching the designs, themes, and storylines of our Disney Parks and Resorts. I then package and present those special perspectives to my fellow Cast Members who, in turn, share the stories with their Guests. Hopefully, I can make it as much fun for them as it has been for me. Oh, something else John Hench once told me, 'You have to know how to have fun—before you can make it for other people.' Frankly, I can't think of anything I'd rather do!"

"Our slogan at Walt Disney Imagineering is 'We Make the Magic!' But I'll let you in on a little secret: I don't believe the magic actually arrives until the moment when the fantasy becomes reality for our guests. Our immersive stories provide wonderful opportunities for our guests to see and do and feel things they could not or would not experience in their everyday lives. They get to fly with Peter Pan over London. They get to climb Mount Everest and have a close encounter with the legendary Yeti. They get to soar over the Golden Gate Bridge on an updraft so powerful that it can lift them away from all of their troubles. I love being an Imagineer because I often get to witness this magical phenomenon and it never fails to remind me of the awesome privilege and responsibility we have.

"Prior to opening Mickey's PhilharMagic at the Magic Kingdom in Walt Disney World, we ran the show for the very first time for a test audience. In the show, stagehand Donald Duck decides to don Maestro Mickey's Sorcerer's Hat and conduct the enchanted orchestra. Without realizing the immense power contained in the hat, things get a little out of control for our con-DUCK-tor. There's a moment when Iago the parrot silently swoops in behind Donald to knock the hat off. I had been worried all along that guests might miss Iago's stealth entrance. But when that moment arrived for our first audience, a little boy shot up from his seat, dropping the walking cane that was propped against his leg brace to the floor. 'Look out, Donald!' he warned as he pointed to the culprit Iago. 'Behind you!' At that moment, the fantasy became real. And it was pure magic."

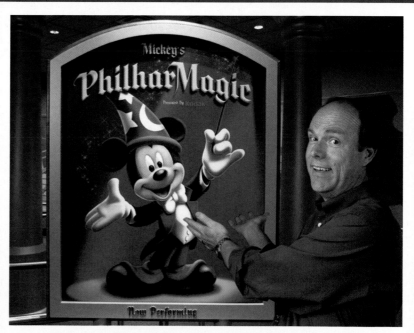

KEVIN RAFFERTY, SENIOR CONCEPT WRITER-DIRECTOR (WDI)

CONNIE VOGT, GUEST SERVICE MANAGER (DLR)

"Sometimes it is the smallest things we do that brightens a Guest's day and makes their experience great. I never expected my actions to have a lasting impact on Madison and I am thrilled that we have stayed in contact over the years."

Connie Vogt, Manager
Disney Clothiers, Ltd.
Disneyland
1313 Harbor Boulevard
Anaheim, CA   92803-6161

Dear Connie:

Your special acts of kindness and caring for one particular young lady, Madison Qualls, have been dramatically brought to my attention. I have shared this account with others who are also impressed with the fact that you would personally relate to one young person's plight, and not treat it as an unfortunate situation that just occurs when you are daily dealing with many people and changing faces.

I am confident from what my granddaughter Madison relates to me that your caring, generous and empathetic behavior is natural. Certainly it is highly commendable. I hope that it gives you real personal satisfaction to know that you have created an enduring positive impression on a bright, properly motivated young lady in her formative years. You have very admirably demonstrated that it is very important to pause in the pursuit of happiness to just make people happy.

Thank you for your kindness and best wishes for your continuing success and personal satisfaction.

Sincerely,

G.J.Mecham

Glenn J. Mecham
Mayor of Ogden, Utah

GJM/cy

"In 1975, I met a little boy I will never forget. He spoke no English and I spoke no Portuguese but we had a wonderful 'Disney Moment.'

"It was early evening, and I was stocking shelves in the Emporium on Main Street, U.S.A. Every time I returned from the stockroom my arms would be full of plush characters and I would play with the children as I loaded up the shelves. I did terrible Mickey impressions, but none of them seemed to care.

"One little boy stayed longer than all the rest and we would act out little scenes with the characters in between my trips to the stockroom. He finally went over to his father and whispered in his ear for a long time, all the while pointing at me. At the end of this whispered conversation, his father burst out laughing. In very heavily accented English he explained that he had told his son that he could have anything he wanted in the store— but just one item. The little boy had just asked for me!"

Nancy Gidusko, Communications (WDW)

ERIC WILLIAMS, HORTICULTURE (WDW)

NANCY GIDUSKO 1975

NANCY GIDUSKO 2005

"When I first started, at the Magic Kingdom, my area was the rose garden. Every morning I would clip the roses and pass them out to the Guests as they walked by. One morning an elderly couple walked up and started talking to me. A year later, the husband returned alone to the rose garden to see me. He wanted to let me know that his wife had passed away, but he had to come and say thank you. He said that during their last year together she often talked about the experience she had at the Magic Kingdom, specifically meeting me and receiving the roses. It showed me that every day I interact with Guests, I never know if it will be their last visit to Walt Disney World and what memories I might help create. By providing our Guests with a world of trees and flowers, I help make sure they are lost in a world of fantasy."

ERIC WILLIAMS

Dear Liz,

My husband and I were at The Living Seas with our daughter and her five children. We were watching Ed Ryan of DiveQuest do his demonstration in the water chamber. When he finished he asked for questions from the audience.

Our oldest granddaughter, Rachel, who is blind since birth, said to me, "I wonder what a wet suit feels like." I asked Mr. Ryan, and he explained everything to Rachel. He let her feel the suit, the breathing apparatus, the mask, all of it. He was great and took a lot of time with Rachel.

After taking pictures, we left the DiveQuest chamber, and soon, Mr. Ryan came looking for Rachel. He invited our family to go behind the scenes of the aquarium, and took us on a very informative tour, showing us how they feed the different kinds of fish.

We went to the top of the fish tanks; saw the dolphin trainers working with the dolphins, feeling the stingrays and all the apparatus used by the divers. Rachel was also allowed to pet a dolphin.

We thanked Mr. Ryan for all the time and attention he gave to Rachel. He really went out of his way to show her and let her "see" everything with her hands. He was absolutely great. Rachel, as a result, had the best time ever. Thank you!

Edward and Maureen Mangan
Clermont, FL.

ED RYAN, LIVING SEAS (WDW)

"I love interacting with children and this young lady was very special — she was discovering Disney through her fingertips. I believe I experience more magic from these special Guest interactions than the Guests do."

GIRISH GULRAJANI
DINING ROOM SERVER
DISNEY WONDER (DCL)

Disney Cruise Vacations:

I would like to express my great delight with the cruise my family took on the Disney Wonder. It was the best cruise I have ever been on.

Of course, the ship itself was beautiful and very clean. Every crew member that we encountered was helpful and courteous. It was definitely a very pleasant experience.

I have to let you know that our dining experience was excellent aboard the ship. Our waiter, **Girish**, was exceptional in every way. He really went out of his way to ensure that our meals were excellent and that we left the table full and satisfied.

I just wanted to share my thoughts. We will have such special memories for years to come.

Lisa G. Wilfong

Gary Stevens
Smithtown, NY 11788

September 26, 2003

To Whom It May Concern:

I want to share some wonderful experiences with you about our Disney cruise and particularly our experiences with a fantastic crew member that we met.

Our time on the Disney Wonder was fantastic. The service, staff and accommodations were just great. Our trip was made even better by our chance encounter with Damien O'Connor, who we met during the first few minutes on the ship. Well, from then on we saw Damien everywhere. He made a visit to our table during my daughter's birthday celebration and often checked in with us just to say "hi" and see how the kids were doing. One evening we returned to our suite and found a signed menu from all the crew delivered by Damien. He gave us the feeling of having our own concierge and did it in a warm, unassuming way. He is a fantastic asset to the Disney Cruise Line and please relay these words to him. He added so much to our trip.

We thank you again for a wonderful vacation experience. Best wishes in the future.

Sincerely,

Gary Stevens

Gary Stevens

DAMIEN O'CONNOR, CREW MEMBER, DISNEY WONDER (DCL)

"While we have responsibility for many Guests, we must never fail to treat each and every adult and child as an individual. I am constantly seeking out Guests to make a 'magical' moment, and when I achieve this I create magic for myself. This makes me proud and genuinely happy to be part of a superb team!"

Above and Beyond

Late in his career Walt Disney said, "I'm not the perfectionist anymore. It's my staff—they're the ones always insisting on doing something better and better." Disney parks and resorts are the kind of environments that, at their best, bring out the best in everyone—Cast Members and Guests alike. An enchantment occurs when the mundane is elevated to the extraordinary by the application of extra steps, extra thoughts, extra efforts—extra attention.

Disney CEO Michael Eisner agrees that striving and aspiring to ever-higher goals is vital to Disney's special sorcery. "Disney has always been known for excellence in all that it does. Our constant eye on quality is reflected in more than the artistry of our animated films or the beauty of our theme parks—it is seen daily in the smiles, thoughtful acts, and generosity of spirit that our Cast Members give to our Guests, creating special memories that last a lifetime."

KIMBERLY CARNE, GUEST RELATIONS (WDW)
"Our Guests have the opportunity to vacation anywhere in the world but choose to come here because of our history and reputation."

FRANCISCO RAMOS
MAIN ENTRANCE OPERATIONS, BLIZZARD BEACH (WDW)
"We have a responsibility to make a difference by creating MAGIC all the time. That is what makes Disney different from other companies. When we exceed our Guests' expectations, they keep coming back again and again."

"I would like to take this opportunity to thank a pair of wonderful Cast Members that helped make a great day even greater. Theses wonderful Cast Members (**Kimberly** and **Francisco**) truly embody the Disney philosophies and I know if Walt were still with us, he would be proud of them."

—Warren S. and Karen R. Allen
Walt Disney World Guests, April 7, 2004

AKIRA MINAMI, FOOD OPERATIONS (TDR)
"In order to provide great Guest service, I maintain a clean and safe work environment and order the best product available for our restaurants."

KOU TERASHIMA, MERCHANDISE PLANNING (TDR)
"I ensure that the shops are stocked with merchandise and the Cast is happy so that they create happiness for our Guests."

Mr. Troy Macklin
Test Track Guest Manager, Epcot
Walt Disney World Co.
P.O. Box 10000
Lake Buena Vista, Florida 32830

Dear Troy,

We want to this take the opportunity to let you know what an outstanding and wonderful employee you have in Greg Balitz who works in "*Fast Pass*" in Epcot. On Monday evening, August 26, 2002, he went above and beyond to make our young daughter happy following an unhappy situation that occurred in Epcot.

When we finished the Body Wars ride and exited the Wonders of Life, we found that someone had stolen our rented stroller. Worst of all, however, was that the stroller had two "masks" that our five-year-old daughter had taken hours to make while walking through the countries of Epcot. She was very upset and crying hysterically.

We met Greg minutes later while on the way to use our Fast Pass tickets for Test Track. He saw how upset our daughter was and inquired as to what happened. When we told him the story he not only offered to go through all of the countries and make her a new mask, but to deliver it to our child during dinner. While eating at the Coral Reef later that evening, Greg delivered our daughter's new mask — complete with birthday greetings and messages from each country——right to our table. Needless to say, our daughter was thrilled!

We think you are very lucky to have such a dedicated and caring employee working for Disney. Mr. Balitz truly reflects the very best that Disney could ever want, and we sincerely hope that his extraordinary kind efforts are appropriately recognized by Disney (*in every way!*).

With thanks,

Janis Feldman

Janis and Greg Feldman

GREG BALITZ, ATTRACTIONS HOST (WDW)
"I take pride and delight in helping our Guests. Providing magical moments gives me satisfaction and joy that cannot be measured. I look forward to providing these experiences daily and I always look for new creative ways to share the magic."

"I remember a boy who was upset and was reminding his father of his promise to let him ride Test Track, but his father was worried about the two-hour wait. I arranged a FASTPASS for them. Guests will write or tell me later that the simple things I do are what they remember most about their entire vacation. I enjoy my job because I have a lot of fun making people happy!"

ELTON GREEN, ATTRACTIONS HOST (WDW)

To Whom It May Concern:

To be completely honest, I am not sure where to even start with this letter other than THANK YOU, THANK YOU, and THANK YOU!!! I can't say enough about how WONDERFUL Disneyland was to us on a recent visit. I am a speech pathologist at an elementary school and on May 31, 2003 my husband and I took two of my students to Disneyland. Their names are Kendal and Nicole, and they are identical seven-year old twins. who have had to overcome many health problems, along with the fact that they are both blind. BUT they are two of the most amazing girls in the world. We know what a wonderful experience Disneyland has always been for us, and we couldn't imagine what it would be like to take these two girls who have never been before.

We arrived at the park in the morning and went to Guest Relations to get a special assistance pass for the girls. We asked them for a Braille map, as the girls are just learning Braille and we thought it would be a good learning experience for them. At first they could not find one. They told me they would find one and wrote down my cell phone number to call me when they did. A short time later, someone from Guest Relations had located a Braille map for the girls!

They could not WAIT to meet all of the princesses. That was all they had talked about since we had discussed going to Disneyland. My husband and I were a little apprehensive about this, since we know how many little girls and boys wait in line to see the princesses and the only reason why that mattered was because Kendal and Nicole can't SEE the princesses. They need extra time so that they can feel the dresses, hair, etc. in order to form their own picture of what the princesses look like.

As we waited in line for the first princess, Ariel, my husband went up to Marcelle and asked him how we could meet other princesses, as he was wearing a button that said 'Ask me about the princesses.' Marcelle was AMAZING! He was so helpful. He came up and introduced himself to Kendal and Nicole and then took them up to meet Ariel. He let them spend extra time with her so they could feel her dress and her hair and talk to her for a minute.

After the girls met Ariel, they were jumping up and down and exclaimed, "Can we meet more princesses?" Marcelle immediately asked us what princesses we wanted to meet and took us around to meet all of them. One by one, the girls got to meet Snow White and Belle. Then Marcelle had us wait by the gate for Cinderella and the girls got some special time with her. Then Cinderella asked the girls to walk her to where she needed to go. This was such a special treat for the girls.

There was one more princess that the girls could not wait to meet. That was Aurora. They were excited because they knew that Aurora had a castle at Disneyland and they couldn't wait to feel it. While we were waiting for Aurora, her special friend Dominique came out and brought the girls a special surprise from Aurora. They were little dolls. Dominique said that this was so the girls could feel Aurora's dress whenever they wanted. HOW SPECIAL!!! Then Aurora came out of the gates and took the girls by the hand and honestly had the biggest heart. She was AMAZING. I could not believe what an amazing job all of the princesses did with the girls. They were so patient and kind and let them feel their faces, hair, dresses, and shoes, even while there was a line a mile long to see them after Kendal and Nicole. They all spent time and talked to the girls and told them stories about their characters.

When Aurora came to get the girls, the girls immediately started asking her many questions. She answered them all so eloquently. She then spent about twenty minutes with the girls. She took them all around her Castle. She had them feel the walls, door, gate, wishing well, statue, and everything else! She was phenomenal. While I walked behind the girls and watched Aurora with them, I couldn't help but wipe away the tears. It just made me so happy that Disneyland has such wonderful people that work for them in providing an experience of a lifetime for everyone! Dominique also was wonderful. She helped to make the time with Aurora special for the girls. When it was time to leave, Aurora, my husband and I could not stop thanking Dominique and Marcelle. Dominique looked at me and said, 'No, thank YOU for opening up our hearts at Disneyland today.' I really could not believe it!!

My husband and I have told everyone of our experience at Disneyland and every time it makes water well up in my eyes as I tell the story of how wonderful every person was that we came into contact with that day. It was a day that I know Kendal and Nicole won't forget, let alone Jeremy and me! I am a teacher of many special needs students and I was so thankful and amazed to see how wonderful your staff was to these two girls. As long as I live I will remember this day and how special Disneyland made us all feel! Thank you so much to everyone for making this wonderful and unforgettable experience!

Sincerely,

Kara and Jeremy Leeper

Kara and Jeremy Leeper

MARCEL SCHMID, CHARACTER DEPARTMENT (DLR)
"I believe in Walt's philosophy — surprise them by giving them more than they expect!"

Dear Mr. Jay Rasulo:

The purpose for contacting you is to acknowledge the tremendous effort of your Disney-MGM Studios Guest Service Manager, Lorraine Oakley, as well as her staff. After an unfortunate incident in the Park, Lorraine went above and beyond her responsibility to ensure our vacation was a truly memorable and magical experience. Because of her care and ultimate Disney spirit, our trip—and more importantly, Lorraine Oakley's kindness—will never be forgotten.

We spent our first of five days in Orlando at Epcot, followed by Disney-MGM Studios. As we walked into MGM, we stopped to put our Park Hoppers in our wallet, took a picture and headed straight to the Rockin' Roller Coaster. As we exited, my fiancé noticed his wallet was missing. The ride staff immediately went into action, led by Ride Manager Mike. Each train was thoroughly combed, and the ride was quickly scanned in and around the track. When Lorraine Oakley arrived she greeted us warmly and assured us the park would do everything possible to assist as best they could.

From this point on, Lorraine stuck to her word. We were escorted to a private lounge in order to make needed phone calls. Deputy Mike Collins from the Orlando Sheriff's Department immediately began taking a lost/stolen report, Disney-MGM Studios Security Manager Kenneth Duren II told us that the Staff would conduct a thorough search of the ride upon the park closing, and Lorraine reproduced our 5-Day Park Hoppers and urged us to return the following day. Little did we know this would only be the beginning of her kindness.

Lorraine contacted us the next morning to make sure we would accept her offer of returning to the park. Within this conversation (and unbeknownst to me), Trevor mentioned that the loss of his wallet had put a damper on the marriage proposal he had planned later in the week. With that said, Lorraine went above and beyond the kindness she had already expressed and quickly arranged the most spectacular proposal that afternoon at the *Beauty and the Beast* Musical, in front of 2000 people! It was a truly magical moment.

To say that Lorraine turned our trip around is an understatement. She has touched our lives in a way that we will never forget. We kept in touch with her for the remainder of our trip and again, to our surprise, she invited us to Pleasure Island to help set off the fireworks. We have never felt so much like a Prince and Princess, but in all thanks to Lorraine and her staff, we felt exceptionally special. She made this milestone event in our lives more enchanting and fairy-tale like than it could have ever been.

The amazing thing about Lorraine and the true reason she should be recognized is the extreme amount of care she shares not only with guests, but with the other Cast Members. She greets each person by first name, exchanging anecdotes or asking questions regarding health, family or events that have recently taken place in their lives. She takes the time to know everyone on a deeper level and for that she is greatly respected by all. On several occasions we were pulled aside and told by Cast Members that Lorraine really embodies what the Disney name is all about. She cares about people. What a rare treasure to find these days. You should feel honored for what she has done and how she has touched Trevor and me. We hope this letter will do what it will to make Lorraine feel as appreciated and special as she made us feel.

All our best,

Nancy Kiss

Nancy Kiss (and Trevor Ziemba)

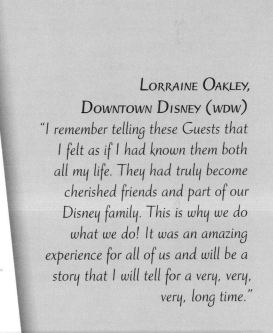

LORRAINE OAKLEY,
DOWNTOWN DISNEY (WDW)
"I remember telling these Guests that I felt as if I had known them both all my life. They had truly become cherished friends and part of our Disney family. This is why we do what we do! It was an amazing experience for all of us and will be a story that I will tell for a very, very, very, long time."

Disneyland
1313 Harbor Blvd.
P.O. Box 3232
Anaheim, CA 92803-3232

To Whom It May Concern:

I would like to give special recognition to Chris Justesen, Food Operations Chef for Disneyland in Anaheim. As a surprise birthday gift for my daughter, I planned a trip to Disneyland. My daughter has Celiac disease. Traveling can be challenging to say the least. I usually travel with her food. However, upon calling Disneyland, Chris displayed an impressive knowledge of gluten-free foods that Celiacs must adhere to, and those menu items that were available throughout the theme park. He even provided a comfort level for me in explaining how the food items are prepared to assure that they did not come in contact with flours that can be toxic to a Celiac.

Unbeknownst to me, the weekend that we were visiting the park was *Spring Break*, yet the supervisor at Tomorrowland (with whom Chris told us to make contact) made us feel as if we were the only ones there. She indicated that she had been *expecting us* and even made a special trip to secure the hot dogs that Callie could eat, plus started the fryer that is *dedicated* for *French fries* only…again extremely important to a Celiac. Callie was served hot dogs and a nice array of fruit and French fries. It made her feel so special to eat a meal at a theme park like everyone else. And Chris came over to make sure that Callie was having a special birthday at Disneyland and that the food was to her satisfaction… and even went on to give her peanut M&M's from his private stash! How "Disney" of him!

Not only was Callie elated to have a day where she was able to just have fun, I also was happy NOT to have to prepare and pack in her food… a nice break for me! Chris followed-up with a call the next week to make sure that our visit was everything that we had anticipated it would be. To say that Chris went above and beyond his role to represent Disneyland and the prevailing attitude of customer service, customer service, and more customer service would be a gross understatement.

So special THANK YOU to CHRIS from two very satisfied customers!!!

Sincerely,

Christine & Callie Davies

CHRIS JUSTESEN, CHEF DE CUISINE (DLR)
"I will do whatever it takes so that Guests with special dietary needs are accommodated and made to feel as if they have no restrictions while visiting the Resort."

September 16, 2004

Dear Mr. Clunie:

I'm writing to let you know about an experience I had at the ESPN Zone last weekend. It started badly, but thanks to your Operations Manager, Richard Stoner, it ended quite differently. A friend invited me to join him at Downtown Disney, where we would get tickets to the Angels game, leaving our cars at the park and taking a shuttle to Anaheim Stadium. A nice plan.

We got to the shuttle pick-up spot at 5:50 p.m. and waited. There were two other couples waiting as well. To make a long story short, the shuttle simply didn't come. The other two couples were very angry and demanded to speak to the manager, who turned out to be Richard. He called the shuttle company many times, to no avail. When no satisfaction could be found with the shuttle, he offered to pay for a taxi to take us to the stadium and make sure that a shuttle would be there for us up at the end. Since the game was about to start at that time and the other two couples were very upset, my friend and I insisted that they take the first taxi to the stadium. Then, just when you think it can't get worse, another taxi could not be found.

This is definitely not a letter of complaint! Rather, I wanted to let you know what an admirable job Richard did in trying to resolve a very difficult situation. When we couldn't get another taxi, he even offered to drive us there in his own car. We decided that was not necessary, but asked if maybe he could just get us a table inside where we could watch the game. Not only did he get us inside, he put us into the Green Room and bought our dinner. The two people who took care of us from that point, Neil and Melissa, treated us like celebrities even though it was quite obvious we were not. It being the end of his shift, Richard was about to leave for the day when this happened. He did not leave! He stayed and took care of the problem from start to finish, sending Gina out with updates while we were waiting at the stop so that we wouldn't feel abandoned. Gina was very professional, as well.

I want you to know that I have a lot of experience with people in the services industries. I know that Richard did not have to do all that he did for us. He didn't even leave until my friend and I were fed and watching a very disappointing game for the Angels. He checked on us from time to time and could not apologize enough. People don't always get that from places that have 'made mistakes' or have problems with customers. Many times they become very rigid and very impolite. We were very impressed with Richard.

I don't know if you get letters like this on a regular basis, but all of the people we dealt with on Saturday stood out as excellent customer service people. I just thought you should know. Please extend our thanks to them all.

Sincerely,

Valerie Lees
Glendora, CA

RICHARD STONER, ESPN ZONE (ANAHEIM)
"We call them 'Guests'—not customers—because they are like Guests in our home and that is how I treat everyone."

The Brooks Family

Walt Disney World Guest Communications
P.O. Box 10,400
Lake Buena Vista, FL 32830

Ladies and Gentlemen:

I am writing to you to give a very hearty 'thank you' to a few of your
wonderful employees due to an event involving my 10-year old daughter,
Megan.

This was our 4th visit to the Disney parks, and my daughter is a HUGE
believer in the characters. During the course of our 4-day stay, she
had managed to acquire a vast amount of autographs from the Disney
characters. Like every little girl, her favorites include all the
princesses, with Ariel being her favorite. She had managed to obtain
all of those, with the exception of Sleeping Beauty and Pocahontas.
But, hands down her all-time favorite characters are Peter Pan and
Wendy.

To make a long story short, I lost my daughter's autograph book two
hours before the park closed on our last day at Disney. You can only
imagine the horror and despair when I discovered it missing. Well, me
and my husband immediately went and bought another book, and had every
intention of spending our remaining two hours in the park trying to
get as many autographs as possible! All I could think of was how in
the world are we going to get anything of value in the remaining time?

We decided to go straight to the Pirate ride, in hopes that Peter Pan
and Wendy would be out and we got lucky, because they were there. Now,
two days had gone by since Meg had last been there, and yet, Peter
remembered Megan! He said, "Hi, Megan, haven't I seen you before?" She
told him yes, but that she had lost her autograph book and was trying
to get all the autographs again. We explained to them that this was
our last two hours in the park.

Peter then brought Karen over, and advised us THEY WOULD PERSONALLY
GET ALL THE AUTOGRAPHS IN THE PARK FOR MEGAN. And instructed us to go
ride attractions and enjoy ourselves for the remainder of our time.
Karen personally took our hotel information and told us she would
contact us later that evening.

At about 10:30 p.m. we received a call from Karen, who was personally
waiting down in the hotel lobby with a package and a letter from
Mickey Mouse himself! I can't even begin to describe the look Megan
got on her face; her eyes just sparkled. Mickey wrote her a letter
stating that Peter Pan had personally flown her autograph book to him
and explained the situation and with much help from his friends, got
as many signatures as possible! If that wasn't enough, the book was
filled from front to back with just about every character imaginable!

Also, these characters didn't just sign their names; a lot of them
included really neat little details or drawings that were unique to
that particular character. It also did not go unnoticed by Megan or us
that some of the signatures were obtained from characters that do not
get 'seen' much in the park, which included Tinker Bell and Jiminy
Cricket, and others that are very unique from the Snow White Queen,
Maleficent, Lady Tremaine and both step sisters from Cinderella.

Also, Peter wrote a special note to Meg at the beginning of her book,
which she can't quit reading or talking about! She now thinks he might
'visit' her through her window some night and whisk her off to
Neverland; too cute! I tried to explain to her that he now lives in
the park at Disney, but she seems to think that he was just visiting
there

You made my little girl's dreams come true in more ways than you could
possibly know.

I do apologize for the lengthy letter her, but I had no other way to
convey the extreme gratitude our family has for what these Disney
employees did. To say they went above and beyond is an understatement!

Thanks so much for everything!

Sincerely,

Dudley and Melody Brooks

Dudley and Melody Brooks
Less Summit, MO

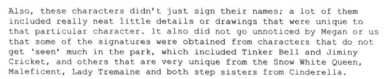

Disneyland Resort
1313 S. Harbor Blvd.
Anaheim, California 92802-3232

RE: Nathan Gebhard

Dear Disneyland Resort:

My family purchased a Hopper package and attended Disneyland and California Adventure from December 13 through 17. On our fourth day, December 16, my family was waiting to enter Disneyland at the front gates. My nine-year-old daughter, Taneal, sat on the side of our double stroller, which slipped from beneath her, and Taneal took a very hard fall to the asphalt. The fall ended up breaking her forearm in two spots. The sight of the bent forearm sent both my wife and I into a small mild shock.

My wife went to get help in this crisis. Within a few seconds, Nathan Gebhard returned to assist and help in any way possible. Nathan quickly returned with a nurse and provided us with help that we desperately needed. Nathan had a nice way about him and diffused a chaotic situation. Taneal and I were assisted to a taxicab where Nathan paid the fare to an Anaheim hospital.

The hospital stay was about seven hours from start to finish. While the doctor was casting her arm, the doctor told us that she was to be on bed rest tomorrow. My daughter's eyes quickly teared up. Taneal was devastated. She still had two days left on her Hopper pass. After the doctor left, I told Taneal that I would bring her back in the near future. This made her very happy.

When we returned to the motel, Taneal and I were amazed to find gifts, autographed pictures, and notes from Cinderella, Sleeping Beauty, and other characters. Nathan had walked over these nice gestures to our motel. Nathan left his cell phone number and asked that we call him and let him know how everything went. Later, I called Nathan and he was wonderful. While speaking with Nathan, I told him of my promise to my daughter to return to Disneyland and asked if there was any way he could help us out with a discounted Hopper package. The next day Nathan delivered no cost Hopper passes for my family.

I cannot express to you how much my family appreciates all that was done for us on our trip. Even with a broken arm, this was a wonderful vacation. Nathan Gebhard made sure that we received the help we needed and went one step further and followed up. I believe Nathan is a very genuine person and you are lucky to have him in your organization. We thank you for your kindness and generosity. Disneyland is a wonderful place and one that we love to return to again and again.

Thank you,

Travis Tanner

Travis Tanner
Washougal, WA

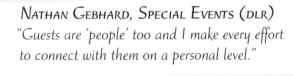

Nathan Gebhard, Special Events (dlr)
"Guests are 'people' too and I make every effort to connect with them on a personal level."

Good Morning,

We are writing to give out highest commendations to two Disney employees. Our family group of eight was visiting the Magic Kingdom. We were spending a week at Walt Disney World to celebrate our parents' (Fred and Mary Burnette) 50th wedding anniversary. Mary had only two wishes: to go on the Haunted Mansion ride, and to meet Happy of the Seven Dwarfs (Happy has been her favorite since the movie came out, and it always disappoints her that Dopey and Grumpy have all the T-Shirts and other promotions). My husband and I went to Guest Services in the morning to find out where and when Happy and the other dwarfs would be doing the meet n' greets and, after they investigated, were told that Happy would only be in the 3 p.m. parade.

About 2 p.m., as we lined up for the parade in front of the Emporium, we discussed ways for Mary to meet Happy either before or after the parade. We decided to find an employee with some authority. We grabbed the next person we saw with a laminated ID badge, who turned out to be Tyson Tinsley, Research Operations Manager for Research and Statistics. We explained our dilemma, and asked if he could find someone to help us. About 15 minutes later, he returned, saying it could be done.

At 3 p.m., we took Fred and Mary with us as Tyson took us over to Guest Services. (They were under the impression they were going to receive something for their anniversary.) Mary was worried that she would miss Happy in the parade, and Tyson reassured her she would not. After a few minutes of waiting, we were taken into a reception room behind the front desk and there, Mary finally met Happy. It probably took several days for the carpet to dry from all the tears that were shed. Mary burst into tears, and several other people in the room cried upon seeing her reaction to the character. Yes, she realizes it's just a 20-something in a big outfit, but she cried anyway. They expressed their love for one another, and they Happy returned to the parade.

On behalf of our entire family, we cannot say enough good about the effort Tyson put into this, as well as that of Maggie Bratcher, who is apparently in charge of the costumed characters. To say that they made Mary's day is an understatement – they made her lifetime. If you have any commendations for efforts above and beyond the call of duty, Tyson and Maggie should definitely receive them.

Sincerely,
Jeff and Sheila Burnette

Tyson Tinsley,
Work Force Planning & Analysis (WDW)
"Our Cast Members are our biggest asset. We have the chance, through our interactions, to make every vacation special for our Guests. It is the Cast Members and the great Guest service that keep our Guests coming back year after year."

Dear Disney,

As I was getting ready to leave the park, I noticed that I was missing a button on my coat. It was night and a button was such a small thing, but I decided to file a report at the Lost and Found center before leaving for Osaka. I had half given up hope, but then I received mail from your company today, only to find my lost button enclosed. Although I had given up on the button, I was suddenly joyous. I was so surprised and delighted. I was very impressed, because after all, they were able to find even one small button due to the many Cast Members cleaning the park constantly. Not even a single bit of trash is ever on the ground. I also work in the services industry and every time I visit TDL, I not only enjoy it thoroughly but also remind myself that I must work as hard as they do. Please continue the wonderful work that you all do. I look forward to visiting again. Thank you very much.

T.Y. 様

"The entire staff on the cruise was the best ever (this was our third cruise in six years). As DVC owners, Castaway Members and dedicated Disney fans, we just wanted you to know that excellent service is what Disney is all about! We look forward to sailing and vacationing with DCL in the future."

Danielle and Jeff Otterson

"Just a short note to thank you for the courtesy with which I was treated last night. My girlfriend lost her purse aboard the Mark Twain, and I was frantic. The whole procedure was handled with dignity and friendliness. I would like to express my gratitude to the numberless smiling employees who treat guests with Walt Disney warmth."

—Mike, August 14, 1966

"I wish I could describe how much joy it brought to my heart to watch you treat my children as though they were as special to you as they are to me. I really can't thank you enough. I honestly had a difficult time describing it to my mom without choking up! I have been to Disneyland at least 20 times and spent my honeymoon at Disney World and this rates as the best experience ever because you were so fantastic to my girls. Thank you, Thank you, Thank you!!!!"

Kathy Jenkins
Disneyland Guest, December, 2003

"My husband and I have always loved coming to Disneyland, but when we first brought our little girls there this spring (then ages 1½ and 3½), it was one of the most memorable experiences for us. Our family has coined the term 'Disneyland Moment'—a moment in time when the parents are so caught up in the emotion of the moment that we are totally teary eyed and have a huge lump in our throat."

—The Bradshaw Family
Disneyland Guests, August 29, 2003

"I am writing to you to express a very personal, heartfelt, deep appreciation for you and all the effort you put forth in your job. I can't even begin to express my gratitude towards you for creating for me the most spectacular, splendid, exhilarating and joyful day I have ever spent. You contribute to a legacy of caring, love and dreams, which each of us take back to our daily lives, to magnify and redistribute to everyone we touch."

—L.C. Johnston, M.D., 1985

46

October 28, 2002

Dear Disney World,

I took my children to the Magic Kingdom today and wanted to thank you for a wonderful "cast member" named Linda at Pirates of the Caribbean. My 5 year old son was very scared by the darkness and started to panic. As we turned to leave, Linda kneeled down and explained that she was a pirate and was not very scary. My son was still not convinced, so she reached into her bag and pulled out a red "gem." She said my son could have it if he went on the attraction and did her a favor. She explained that she had three dogs and two cats and had lost them—could he look for them while on the ride and make sure they were okay. My son clutched the gem in his hand and had a wonderful time on the ride, finding all three dogs and two cats. When we exited, Linda was there and told him he had earned the treasure as she wished us a wonderful day.

I have been to many theme parks and can honestly say that this is the first time I remember an employee going out of their way to make a visitor feel special. My son is still happily clutching that gem in his hand, even though he is fast asleep in bed now. Linda was absolutely wonderful - she really made a difference to us today!

J. Couto

"I love what I do and I thoroughly enjoy making magic for our Guests. When I make a Guest feel special or help a child overcome their fear, I experience some Disney Magic of my own."

LINDA ARCHER, ATTRACTIONS HOSTESS (WDW)

Mr. Tom McAlpin
Disney Cruise Line
210 Celebration Place, Suite 400
Celebration, Florida 34747

Dear Mr. Tom McAlpin:

I have always heard that the Disney Corporation trains their employees to give the ultimate service to their customers. Our family experienced that unparalleled service on a recent Disney Wonder cruise. Both the children and adults in our family were made to feel very important and individually special. We had a wonderful cruise and enjoyed every minute. Beyond that I must share the thoughtfulness and generosity of one of the Disney Wonder employees. This person went far beyond even the Disney expectations for service.

The last night of our cruise we prepared for the next day knowing we needed to set out clothes to wear for the next day and "bags in the hall by 11 p.m." As the eight other family members enjoyed the Farewell Party, I stayed and got things ready. The family returned, and we put our bags out and went to sleep. I awoke at 2:30 a.m. and saw the two piles of clothes laid out for my husband and me and realized I had no slacks to wear home. I must have packed them in the suitcase!

In a panic I awoke my husband. He went to Customer Service to see if he could find our suitcases. He was told that would be an impossible task. Trying to figure out how to help me he was overheard by one of your crew members, Boris Rincic.

Asking my size, he offered to see if a pair of his slacks would fit me. Boris went to his quarters and brought back a pair of slacks for me to try. My husband offered to pay for them, but he would not take anything. He just asked to have them sent back to him. My husband brought them back to me—they fit perfectly. I wore them all the way home and they matched the jacket I was wearing!

I am sending them back to Boris with much gratitude. He saved the day for me in what could have been a very embarrassing situation. He literally gave the 'shirt off his back,' but in this case, his slacks.

That is certainly one of the most gracious and thoughtful acts I have ever experienced. Thank you for employing such considerate and gracious people.

Sincerely,

Carole Matthes

Carole Matthes
Lincoln, NE

cc: Captain John Barwis
      Boris Rincic, Engine Department

BORIS RINCIC,
ENGINEERING, DISNEY WONDER (DCL)

CATHY CLAYPOOL, LEFT, COLLEGE PROGRAMS COORDINATOR (WDW)
LISA MILLER, RIGHT, GUEST RELATIONS (WDW)

"The following is a magical moment that touched my heart and is one I will always remember.

"Harry and Shirley were Annual Pass Holders who had been coming to Walt Disney World since 1980. Epcot was their favorite park and not a Wednesday would go by without a visit. They were an elderly couple who brought wooden gifts during the holidays for Cast Members throughout the park. They had always commented on how good we treat our senior citizens and that we were their 'family.'

"We really are a family, a diverse family that is comprised of many different people from around the world working as one and touching lives forever—people just like Harry and Shirley.

"It was about this time two years ago that Shirley found out that she was fighting cancer. Harry reached out to his Epcot family for support and prayers. During Shirley's last hospital stay, Lisa Miller from Guest Relations and I went to the hospital to visit Shirley at her bedside. If she couldn't come to Disney we wanted to bring Disney to her. She loved her Epcot family and we loved her. A few days later Shirley passed away. We made her day but she definitely left a bright spot in our life. This is what the MAGIC is all about.

"Harry still visits every Wednesday and remains eternally grateful for all that we have done. We all miss Shirley."

CATHY CLAYPOOL
COLLEGE PROGRAMS COORDINATOR (WDW)

Marché S. Heath

Walt Disney World
Guest Communications
P.O. Box 10040
Lake Buena Vista, FL 32830-0040

Dear Guest Relations Management:

My family and I visited Walt Disney World for the first time a month ago. We had a great six day family vacation! One of the highlights of our trip was our experience at the Hollywood and Vine Restaurant at your Disney-MGM Studios.

Sandy (not sure of last name) was our server and she was very friendly. She went out of her way to help us with our son's finicky food choices. She did it all with a genuine smile and a heart to please. She actually took time to get to know a little about us. When we left the restaurant we felt like we had visited with family. We even exchanged hugs.

As we went through the buffet line a second time, one of the cooks, Michael (not sure of his last name) asked how we liked the food. Well, we do A LOT of buffets and Hollywood and Vine has one of the best variety and food we have ever had. So I shared that with Michael and he said, "We aim to please." We were very pleased.

The third time up to the buffet, Michael also asked us some "get to know you" questions. I asked him if he could tell me the ingredients in the creamed corn spoon bread. He did better than that; he said, "I will give you the recipe." He ended up giving me *three* recipes. He even went a step further by having the head chef break down a recipe that is usually made for hundreds to a serving size for a family. I was shocked. Restaurants rarely share recipes; this was beyond the call of duty.

These two employees should be recognized for the exceptional way they carried out their jobs. Thank you Hollywood and Vine for helping to make this vacation one to remember.

Sincerely,

Marché Heath

Marché S. Heath

SANDY COX, FOOD & BEVERAGE (WDW)
"I enjoy what I do, especially interacting with the children. I always ask them to tell me something special about their hometown and they usually have great stories to share."

Dear Ms. Deese-Byrnes:

Recently my family enjoyed a week-long stay at Old Key West, and we had such an extraordinary experience that wanted to share it with you in hopes that your fine employees might be recognized for their commitment to the 'Magical' experience that Disney promises you when you stay on Disney properties.

Before we arrived, my wife and I were concerned about our daughter Allison's allergy to dairy products and how we would deal with this during our stay at Disney. Allison is allergic to eggs, milk, peanut butter and other dairy byproducts. My wife called and spoke with several Disney employees who promised her it would be all right, but we were still nervous about how it would all work out.

Our first night at Old Key West, we chose to have dinner at Olivia's Café and your chef, Kenny Boston, personally came to our table and showed us an allergy sheet that included the ingredients of all the meals served in the Café, along with his personal guarantee that her meal would be safe for her to eat.

In all the years that we have been dealing with her allergies, it is rare that a chef would take the time to visit with us and reassure us, let alone work with us and help prepare a meal that is satisfying and enjoyable for Allison to eat. You can imagine the anxiety that comes with the fear of an allergic reaction during a meal, and not being at home to deal with it at all.

Service from your wait staff was no different than our experience with Kenny. Karen Rushlow served us breakfast every morning during our stay and she was wonderful. We had all the confidence in the world that Karen would make certain that Alison's meal was safe for her to eat. She asked questions about her needs and made sure that Alison's experience was safe and enjoyable. Karen would pick up on the little things and remembers them from day to day.

We are so accustomed to people being inconsiderate and uncooperative when it comes to Alison's allergies that we don't expect things to be any different when we go out to eat. To have Kenny and Karen show so much care and concern for our daughter's allergies; Lori and I were deeply touched. We look forward to staying with you again in the future.

After our stay with you at Old Key West we joined the Vacation Club upon arriving at home. The girls are still asking us when we can go back to visit. It truly lived up to the 'Home away from home' advertising that you promise.

Best,
Brent A Cross, CPCU, ARM
Bangor, Maine

"The lady Cast Member at Sinbad's Seven Voyages was so kind to talk to me in sign language—very slowly, as she told me a story of magic. When my little sister asked her how she was able to communicate with me (because my sister does not know sign language), the lady replied, 'I used a little magic.' She then gave my sister a sticker and told her that it will help her speak to me someday.

"Thank you so much for the tons of happiness you brought to me! My happiness knows no bounds!"

—*Tokyo DisneySea Guest*

KENNY BOSTON, CULINARY,
DISNEY'S OLD KEY WEST RESORT (WDW)
"I really enjoy dealing with Guests one-on-one, and their satisfaction and happiness is my motivation to go above and beyond."

Touching Lives

Bob Iger, Disney's president, chief operating officer and CEO-elect, believes that "everything Disney stands for—our traditions, heritage, and values—is embodied in our dedicated worldwide Cast. The spirit of Disney lives within these men and women who welcome our Guests into realms of fantasy and imagination, helping them forget the hurried pace of the outside world by making that extra effort to reach out in special, meaningful, and often unexpected ways."

There are so few jobs and careers that give an individual the opportunity to meet people on the threshold of their dreams, but Disney Cast Members have this indulgence every day.

There's a spark when a thoughtful action, an extra effort, or a kind word creates a life-altering moment for that Guest. . . .

But Cast Members should be careful—when they wittingly or unwittingly touch the life of a Guest, they may wind up with the greater reward!

Pat Moss

Manager
Disneyland Resort Guest Relations
Box 3232
Anaheim, CA 92803

Dear Sir or Madam:

My 11-year-old granddaughter and I spent five days in Disneyland the week before Christmas. I had been apprehensive about the trip because she is profoundly deaf and it is difficult for me to communicate with her.

I called your Guest Relations Office before we left because I read where you offer interpreters for the deaf. That's the way Jordan and I became acquainted with Rebecca Visca. She turned out to be one of the highlights of our entire Disneyland experience.

Rebecca planned every detail out with me before our visit so I was comfortable with meeting places, times, etc. We spent one entire day (our first day) together in the park, and every detail went smoothly. She even made sure that we were in a spot for the fireworks where Jordan could "experience" the snow at the end of the show.

I was concerned about how Jordan would relate to her because she's been reluctant to speak in the hearing world for the past few months. Well, I don't know how anyone can not respond to Rebecca's personality. Jordan and I fell for her at first sight!!

I have many memories of my trips to Disneyland—this is the second granddaughter I have taken. However, none of them are more precious to me than the day Rebecca devoted to seeing Jordan was able to enjoy the park to its fullest.

Thank you for making this service available.

Sincerely yours,

Pat Moss
Yakima, WA

REBECCA VISCA, GUEST RELATIONS (DLR)
"Every Guest is unique and special and I try to make their visit memorable. With my sign language interpreting, they experience the shows through me. It is really rewarding to touch their lives in a special way and to share something that they may not have experienced otherwise."

"Back in 1987 I decided to proactively pursue my lifelong goal of working at Walt Disney Imagineering. I began by developing a concept for a new attraction with the intent of somehow getting it into the hands of the powers that be at WDI and thus wow them by my theme park design brilliance. I treated the whole process as if I was really working at WDI on an actual project. I worked eight hours a day (in addition to my regular job) and made drawings, sketches, plans, paintings, scripts, costumes, music, models, the whole shebang. Three years and hundreds of designs later the end was in sight. I had created five complete attractions from scratch and was working on a scheme to get them up to Walt Disney Imagineering in Glendale, when all of the sudden, as if by magic (and in typical Disney fashion), WDI announced the Sorcerer's Apprentice Program. A Disney attraction design competition open to Disneyland and Walt Disney World cast members only, with the grand prize being an internship at WDI! I was in the Disneyland Entertainment Department at the time and saw this as the opportunity I'd been looking for. The competition was limited to one entry per person—so I had to choose which of the five designs I would submit. After agonizing over it I went with 'Great Escapes,' an Indiana Jones™-type runaway jeep ride (I had no idea WDI was working on an actual Indy attraction at the time). Well, at the end of the day, with over 400 submissions, I was fortunate to be chosen as the grand-prize winner. I got the internship and 15 years later I'm still here. So I guess, in true Disney fashion, I lived happily ever after. Oh, and then I actually got to work on the real Indiana Jones™ attraction, icing on the cake."

DAVE DURHAM, DIRECTOR, CONCEPT INTEGRATION (WDI)

"There is really no secret about our approach. We keep moving forward—opening up new doors and doing new things, because we are curious. And curiosity keeps leading us down new paths. We're always exploring and experimenting. We call it 'Imagineering'—the blending of creative imagination with technical know-how."

—Walt Disney

"My wife and I were most impressed with the imagination that went on in the development of Disneyland as well as the color, the vivid detail and the hours of effort in making Disneyland one of the finest attractions in the world."

—JJ Rutherford
July 17, 1963

"Imagination, solicitude for details, and the most exquisite attention to the creation of the illusion everywhere."

—D. Fraser
April 23, 1969

Dear Maggie (At First Aid):

I want to thank you for the kindness you extended to my boys and me during out recent trip to Disneyland.

Shortly after arriving back at Disneyland Saturday night, my 9-year old Timothy got a stomach ache. I didn't know what to do as we were all so excited and set to spend our late evening of our trip at the Park. My brother, Arved, was traveling with us, so I sent him and my other two sons into the Aladdin Play, allowing me 15 minutes to figure out what to do. I was hopeful his stomach ache would pass; however, Timmy's pain did not go away so I sent my brother on Pirates with William, my 7-year old son. My 11-year old Jonathan would not go on the ride because, "Mom, I could not enjoy the ride knowing that Timmy is suffering." So, Jon and I brought Timmy into the First Aid Station.

You greeted Tim at the door and were so cute with him. He was given a place to rest with a blanket to keep him warm. After 20 minutes or so, he *did* start feeling better. You then gave us two "backdoor" passes which created so much excitement for my boys (and their mother!). We could hardly wait to meet William and Arved, and share out great news with them. We talked about rides and decided which ones to ride. We had SO MUCH FUN! After riding the Matterhorn and Rocket Rods, the boys wanted to go back to the First Aid Station to tell "that nice nurse" which rides we chose. I wish you could have seen what these two passes meant to my three sons and my brother. Instead of staying until midnight, we left for our hotel a little after 8:00 because Timmy was not feeling well. We left happy and so excited thanks to your kindness.

You made such a difference for me that night. I can't tell you what it meant to have those special passes and how much fun and excitement that generated for all of us. I know that Saturday night is very busy – perhaps the busiest day of the week. I was deeply touched. Your kindness made a substantial difference in our lives. Thank you.

We will be there again next March for our annual trip!

With love,

Sylvia Fenton

Sylvia Fenton

MARGARET CLARK, GUEST HEALTH NURSE (DLR)
"Receiving this letter is my favorite memory as a Cast Member. It is fun to relive this special Guest interaction whenever I think of this family. I hope to see them again on their next visit to the Resort."

Dear Disneyland Paris,

I feel that I should write and give you a very big thank you. I am a support worker/communicator/guide and I work with people who are deaf and blind. I recently came on a holiday with a man I work with called David. He is 34 and has been deaf and blind from a very early age and until about four months ago knew absolutely nothing about Disney at all.

On entering the parks, we were given a facility pass which helped a great deal. David was also given a Braille embossed copy of some information about Disney, which was brilliant, and made him feel part of it.

I could honestly go on and on. It was an amazing experience for David and me. I felt very honored that I was chosen to introduce a world he knew nothing about. He got very attached to the characters and of course they should be applauded for their patience and understanding.

I would think a park with your reputation gets quite a lot of thank you letters, but this one is more than that. Thank you very much for such a fantastic time!

Thank you again,
J-J
Support Worker
UK

CLIVE ROBESON
DISNEY'S HOTEL NEW YORK
(DLRP)
"I provide that Disney touch that makes even the most delicate situations an opportunity to shine and maintain our image. We have only one goal—excellence!"

EMILE PECORARO, CHEF, ESPN CLUB (WDW)
"As a child watching the Wonderful World of Disney every Sunday night, I could only imagine what a special place Disneyland was and still is today. My family and I had the opportunity to come to Walt Disney World on vacation in 1981. What an experience! We left with so many fond memories of the 'magic' provided by the Cast, we knew we had to come back. I would never have dreamed that one day I would have the opportunity to provide our Guests with the same 'magic,' it is a privilege to be part of Walt Disney's dream!"

2005   1981

BRUCE KIMBRELL, MAIN ENTRANCE/GUEST SERVICES (DLR)
"When I was a supervisor in Fantasyland I spent a morning assisting a terminally ill child: a five-year-old girl who had wished for some private time with Minnie Mouse. We had arranged for her to meet with Minnie at Minnie's House in the newly built Mickey's Toontown. When Minnie approached the little girl and bent down to hug her in her wheelchair, the little girl hugged back and said, "I love you." I could hear the character Cast Member begin to cry. I cried too. It was proof to me that dreams are reality."

Dear Mr. Disney:

"I want to tell you how impressed I was with the attitude of all the employees at Disneyland. They seem to be the most pleasant, courteous, and happy group of people that I have ever run into. My sincerest wishes for your continued success, and a happy, prosperous New Year."

Otis, January 5, 1966

"Beside the fact that Disneyland is so clean and fun, the thing we were most impressed with was the attitude of all the employees. Throughout the day, each worker was doing so much more than their job. They all had big smiles and were so kind. Our day at Disneyland will stand out as one of the highlights of our life."

C. Seamons, May 1989

"Magic Kingdom is very underrated. It is superb on all accounts—Quality All The Way—and the operators were genuinely friendly and seemed eager to make our stay a memorable one. I wish to remain anonymous so your staff will know the sincerity with which we thank you and all those connected with Disneyland."

Disneyland Guest, June 15, 1963

"I have visited Cedar Point, Kings Island, Bo-Lo Island and other parks in the Midwest, but this was my first experience with Disneyland. I don't know how you do it, but the morale of your staff and their dedication to showing the guests a great time is amazing! This goes right down to the sweepers, who were right on top of a falling ice cube, sweeping it well before it had a chance to melt!"

J. M. Lenard, January 1988

MARTHA, 1973

MARTHA BLANDING, MERCHANDISE SPECIAL EVENTS (DLR)

"I often tell this story about a chance encounter I had with a young Guest that affected us both at different times and in different ways. When I was a Tour Guide in the early 70s, I remember meeting a young girl while waiting for my group in New Orleans Square. Though she was not on my tour, we chatted about the Park and about my role in Guest Relations. As I recall, she asked a lot of questions and was very curious about me.

"Fast-forward 20 years later and I am working in Merchandise Special Events planning a function for the Disney University. I am discussing final arrangements over the phone, when the Disney University Cast Member tells the story of when she was a Guest in the Park and we met in New Orleans Square. I could not believe it—she was the little girl! She stated that I had left such a positive impression on her that day, she wanted to be just like me. She also stated that it was because of me that she had become a Cast Member at Disneyland.

"I was so shocked, I thought for sure she had the wrong Martha. I asked if she knew who I was, and she said, 'Yes I do.' It is not every day that you learn someone aspires to be like you—what an honor. It is hard to believe that a simple conversation could have left such an impact, but I will always remember this young lady and how special she made me feel. It goes to prove that every day; we have an opportunity to leave lasting impressions upon our Guests through the 'simple things' we do."

From the Desk of
Vinnie and Mary Del Borrello

Dear Dean Gaschler,

On behalf of the happiest Grand Marshals you'll ever encounter, I wish to thank you for taking such good care of my gang!

During our first conversation, you told me that you would do your best to make my dear friend Deputy Daniel Hodess's time in the park unforgettable! Your commitment to doing just that was quite evident! He had an incredible time, as did the rest of us! I believe we all sprained our faces from smiling so much!

Like so many other people, I am a huge Disney lover! I have been going to Disney World since the day it opened. BUT, nothing will equal the enormous feeling of pride I had on September 9th, 2000 when I saw Danny's smiling face while waving to the layers of people standing on the parade route.

Nothing will match the look of surprise when he heard his name booming over the loud speakers as we turned down Main Street. And nothing will ever compare to the joy on his face when we reached the end of the line and were greeted by the beautiful harmony of the Dapper Dans and the clever wit of Miss Tabby. Those shared moments will stay with me forever.

Dean, I understand that both the Dapper Dans and Miss Tabby really went out of their way to visit with our party. I would greatly appreciate it if you would pass along a sincere thank you to both the Dapper Dans and Miss Tabby. They are all to be commended for making Danny's day special!

Last, but certainly not least...Dean, you are an absolute gem! It was definitely my pleasure meeting you. You are a gracious gentleman and in my humble opinion, you are the 'perfect man' for the job! That smile never left your face...I think you enjoyed the experience almost as much as we did.

I hope our paths will cross again someday. Either way, you will always hold a special place in my heart for what you did for all of us, but most importantly, Danny.

Warmest Regards,

Mary Del Borrello

Mary Del Borrello
Davie, FL

I would like to take this opportunity to thank you for what you did for my wife, my friends and myself. As you were made aware of some of the incidents that occurred to me, you made my hard work worth while. It took a lot of little steps to make the trip possible for me. Part of my goal was to show my wife that we could still do things that are enjoyable and that we can still have fun.

I wish to commend you and the staff that took the time to share that moment of our honorary positions with us. You made it a very special occasion one that we will cherish for a long time. Thanks again to you and all the staff involved.

Daniel Hodess

Daniel Hodess

Dean Gaschler
Grand Marshall Coordinator (wdw)
"On Saturday, September 9, 2000, I selected Dan Hodess, his family and friends to be the Grand Marshals of the Magical Moments Parade. Dan is a Deputy Sheriff of Broward County. About two years ago, while assisting a motorist, Dan was struck by a car and lost both of his legs. Through numerous surgeries and countless hours of therapy, Dan had a goal of walking the Disney Theme Parks and playing golf on a Disney course. He was here celebrating his miraculous achievement."

Walt Disney World Guest Communications
P.O. Box 10,000
Lake Buena Vista, FL 32830

Mr. Lee Cockerell,

I was a very recent guest to the Walt Disney World Resort. I come to Disney World at least once a year, and I must say this was by far the most "magical" trip that I have ever had. I would like to take a moment and mention the reason why it was so memorable, and why I will continue to come back year after year.

About two months ago I had been in contact with your wedding department looking for a good way to propose to my then girlfriend in Disney World. I was told there was no department to really help out planning an engagement but I was transferred to a lady named *Cara Lynn Moccia*. She put me at ease and gave me some very good ideas. Throughout the next two or three weeks we decided a way to propose and made arrangements to meet in the park and get it done.

Now I know a little about how Disney works, and how they create magical moments for their guests, but I must say this was more of a magical day. I was to propose on Valentines Day, and that morning I found an envelope under my hotel door. To my amazement I found two one-day park hopper tickets for me and my girlfriend given by Cara Lynn. I found out a little later she did this around 1:00 am that morning (AMAZING DEDICATION). We arrived at the Magic Kingdom and I met up secretly with Cara Lynn to finalize all plans for the proposal. She managed to hold us seats on the curb on Main Street for the 3 PM parade and that's where the magic really began.

Right before the parade she pulled me out of the crowd (all planned) and she had a poster made that read "Hey Beth Will You Marry Me?" She asked the crowd for the parade to read out loud and to my girlfriend's surprise I got on my knee and asked if she would marry me. After saying yes, Cara Lynn, with the help of *T.D. Hoines*; Magic Kingdom Main Street Operations, and *Chris Itrato*: Magic Kingdom merchandise, we were showered with Disney gifts. Bride and groom Mickey ears, bride and groom Mickey and Minnie stuffed animals, a signed drawing of Sleeping Beauty and Price Philip made out to us, front of the line passes, a private meet and greet with my now-fiancée's favorite character, Mary Poppins, a signed autograph book of all different characters—all to melody of our own barber shop quartet singing to us.

This was an incredibly orchestrated event for me by all involved, Cara Lynn, T.D. Haines, and Chris Itracto. Cara Lynn is one of those people that I think I will always remember, and you should feel very lucky to have her as part of your team. She went way above and beyond for me and made it the most "magical" day of my life.

Sincerely,

Michael P. Williams
Woodbury, New Jersey

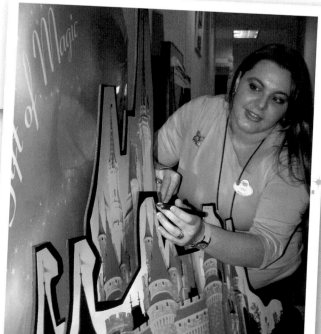

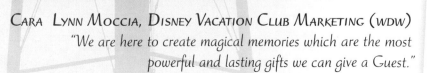

Cara Lynn Moccia, Disney Vacation Club Marketing (WDW)
"We are here to create magical memories which are the most powerful and lasting gifts we can give a Guest."

KAREN ACKLEY, STORE OPERATIONS (DLR)

MARY TIERNEY, MAIN STREET STORES (DLR)
"This was something we did as a team to create a moment of happiness in the boy's life."

"I have known since my first day as a Cast Member in 1976 that I was 'walking in Walt's footsteps.' This is a story I use as an example of our Cast Member heritage when I facilitate the 'Walt & You' class and is a memory that will live in my heart forever.

"In 1984, a father involved in a bitter custody battle poured kerosene throughout a Buena Park motel room, lit a match, and ran outside leaving his seven-year-old son, David, inside. The story made headlines around the world.

"David survived but experienced incredible injuries and permanent disfigurement. After numerous skin grafts and painful surgeries, he was allowed rare moments outside, and David's wish was to go to Disneyland!

"Word spread quickly on the day of his visit. This incredible little boy was here! David was accompanied by his mother and a friend... no fanfare. When word of his arrival reached the Emporium where I was a supervisor, a fellow Cast Member, Mary Tierney, said to me, 'We have to do something for him!' Money was collected and gifts were purchased. I found out when and where David would be, and Irene Pfieffer, who has since retired, and myself were to present the gifts to David. We didn't know how we were going to get through this, as we are both mothers.

"We waited on Main Street, below the window of Walt Disney's apartment. Then we saw them; his mother was pushing his wheelchair. David was a small boy wrapped in the special bandages, and all we could see were his eyes and mouth.

"We walked up to him and, leaning down, I told him, 'David, you see that big building (the Emporium) behind you? All the people who work there are your friends and they wanted you to have these special souvenirs of your visit to Disneyland.' His lips could barely move, but we heard a faint 'thank you.' We waved good-bye and Irene and I stepped backstage where our emotions could finally be released. We just held each other and cried."

—*Karen Ackley*

HONG KONG DISNEYLAND

Matt Holding, Task Force (DLR)
"I am so proud to be able to spread the Disney magic around the globe. As I walk around the Hong Kong Disneyland site, I cannot help but be swept away to 1955. Hong Kong Disneyland will truly be a place that will be a crossroads for Asian and Western cultures to unite and deliver a world-class entertainment experience."

Jerome Ip, Food and Beverage (HKDL)
"When I saw the site for the first time from the shuttle bus on the way to my interview, I remember thinking, WOW! People are going to get so blown away by this! I want to be part of it!"

From its shaky and humble beginnings in reclaimed orange and walnut groves in Anaheim to ten parks in three countries—and another to join the family soon—we can hear, if we only open our hearts and open our minds, and listen with all our senses intact, the echoes across the decades. These vibrations will resonate within our spirits and inform our future in service to this great and influential community of shared dreams and aspirations for true humanity.

In one of his final interviews, Walt discussed, again in his own humble and forthright way, the legacy he would leave. His ideas are as true today as they were when Disneyland first opened. These ideas will remain the foundation of the Cast Members' philosophy, for decades to come.

"Well, I think that by this time my staff, my young group of executives, and everything else, are convinced that Walt is right!" he said. "That quality will out. And so I think they're going to stay with that policy, because it's proved that it's a good business policy. Give the people everything you can give them. Keep the place as clean as you can keep it. Keep it friendly, you know. Make it a real fun place to be. I think they're convinced, and I think they'll hang on after. . . as you say . . . well . . . after Disney."

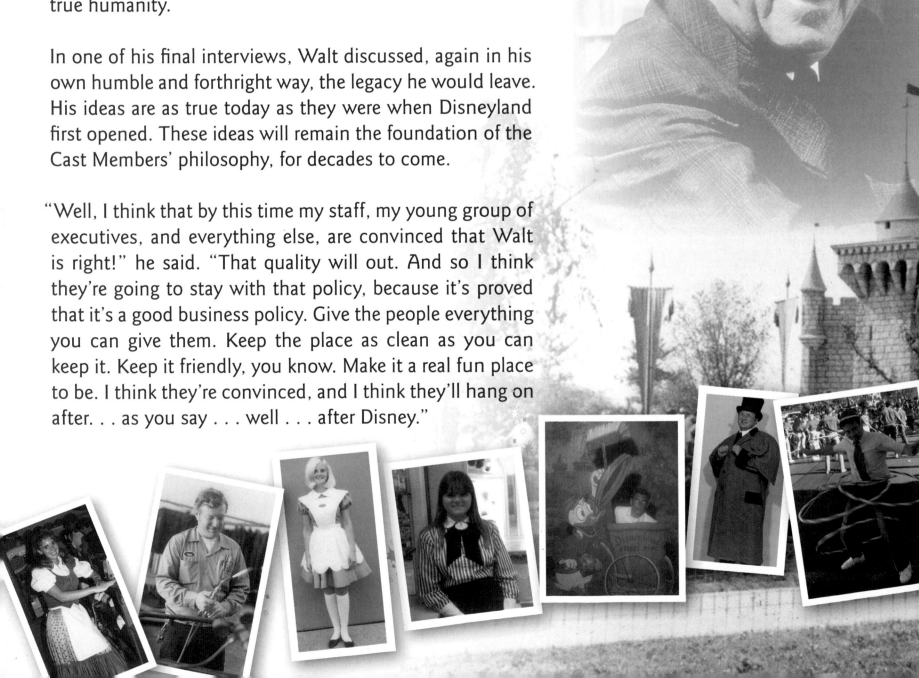

BELOW: Walt Disney reads the Fantasyland Dedication on Opening Day, July 17, 1955.

BOTTOM: Smiles all around!

On the tenth anniversary of Disneyland, Walt cautioned his Cast Members: "I just want to leave you with one thought: that it's just been sort of a dress rehearsal . . . So if any of you start resting on your laurels, I mean, just forget it, because—the show goes on tomorrow." This was true four decades ago, it remains true today.

Our first fifty years are just a beginning. As we continue to expand the exceptional standards and outstanding legacy of Walt Disney Parks and Resorts throughout the world, we can never rest on past accomplishments, and never forget the traditions of quality established a half century ago.

This is a legacy of distinction that you carry on every day, in everything that you do at Disney. For this extraordinary commitment, I sincerely thank you.

This story of Cast Member excellence does not end here; this is just the beginning. The rest of the story is for us to write.

—Jay Rasulo